Nuts

ABOUT

Nuts

Michael Rosen

Illustrated by
SAMI SWEETEN

PictureLions
An Imprint of HarperCollinsPublishers

Also by Michael Rosen and Sami Sweeten
Freckly Feet and Itchy Knees

First published in hardback in Great Britain by
HarperCollins Publishers Ltd in 1993
10 9 8 7 6 5 4 3 2 1
First published in Great Britain in Picture Lions in 1994
10 9 8 7 6 5 4 3 2 1
Picture Lions is an imprint of the Children's Division,
part of HarperCollins Publishers Limited,
77-85 Fulham Palace Road, Hammersmith,
London W6 8JB
ISBN 0 00 193528 3 (Hardback)
ISBN 0 00 664054 0 (Picture Lions)
Produced by HarperCollins Hong Kong
This book is set in Educational Baskerville

I dream of ice cream
ice cream's a wow
ice cream's cool
I want some now

I scream for ice cream in the garden
I scream for ice cream on a tray
I scream for ice cream tomorrow
I scream for ice cream today

give a scoopful to a cat
give a scoopful to a baby
give a scoopful to a dog
give a scoopful to a lady

ice cream in a cake
ice cream in a cup
ice cream on the table
ice cream piled up

grab a slab for the outing
grab a slab for the fair
grab a slab for the playground
grab a slab for the bear

don't dance on your ice cream
don't fling your ice cream
don't sleep on your ice cream
don't sling your ice cream

lick it
nuzzle it
feel it
guzzle it

I'm funny about honey
honey is sweet
hand me the honey
honey's a treat

I want honey in my tummy with raisins
I want honey in my tummy on the train
I want honey in my tummy on the bus
I want honey in my tummy on the plane

give a dollop to a mermaid
give a dollop to a snowman
give a dollop to a goblin
give a dollop to a showman

honey in a tub
honey in a jar
honey in my hair
honey in the car

lug a tub to the forest
lug a tub to your tent
lug a tub to the game
lug a tub to the event

don't bath in your honey
don't attack your honey
don't roll in your honey
don't smack your honey

pour it
smear it
love it
cheer it

I'm nuts about nuts
nuts are great
crack seven
crack eight

chuck me a nut in my hut
chuck me a nut at the zoo
chuck me a nut in my bucket
chuck me a nut in the loo

give a bagful to a jockey
give a bagful to a plumber
give a bagful to a crab
give a bagful to a drummer

nuts in the papers
nuts in a stew
nuts in a bowling alley
nuts in some glue

pack a packet in your luggage
pack a packet in your pocket
pack a packet in your rucksack
pack a packet in your rocket

don't choke on that nut
don't sit on that nut
don't gallop on that nut
don't spit on that nut

choose it
tap it
crack it
rap it

I'm always awake for cake
cake is the tops
cut me some
cut me lots

make a cake like a truck
make a cake like a house
make a cake like a computer
make a cake like a mouse

give a chunk to a monkey
give a chunk to a fighter
give a chunk to a donkey
give a chunk to a writer

cake with candles
cake with a cherry
cake on a speedboat
cake on a ferry

take a cake to a camp
take a cake to a cook-out
take a cake to a concert
take a cake to a lookout

don't squeeze your cake
don't soak your cake
don't rub your cake
don't poke your cake

mix it
bake it
cut it
break it

I've got a head for bread
bread is nice
slice it once
slice it twice

spread that bread with a knife
spread that bread with a spoon
spread that bread with a fork
spread that bread very soon

give a slice to your sister
give a slice to your brother
give a slice to your teddy
give a slice to your mother

bread in your lunchbox
bread on a poster
bread in a pudding
bread in the toaster

feast on a piece in the rain
feast on a piece in the snow
feast on a piece in the castle
feast on a piece at the show

don't wear your bread
don't lie on your bread
don't stamp on your bread
don't cry on your bread

cut it
tear it
gobble it
share it

I've got the legs for eggs
eggs are heaven
grab six
grab seven

beg for an egg with beans
beg for an egg with cheese
beg for an egg with ham
beg for an egg with peas

give a bit to your dolly
give a bit to your teacher
give a bit to a ghost
give a bit to a creature

eggs in an omelette
eggs in a roll
eggs in eggcups
eggs in a bowl

bite into the white in space
bite into the white on a trip
bite into the white on a bench
bite into the white on a ship

don't drop that egg
don't punch that egg
don't kick that egg
don't crunch that egg

boil it
beat it
fry it
eat it

I want my rice in a trice
rice is wild
I want a heap
I want a pile

fry some rice with sauce
fry some rice with corn
fry some rice with peppers
fry some rice with a prawn

give a spoonful to a parrot
give a spoonful to a waiter
give a spoonful to a martian
give a spoonful to a skater

rice in a salad
rice in a canoe
rice at a wedding
rice in your shoe

try some rice in the street
try some rice at school
try some rice at the beach
try some rice at the pool

don't flick your rice
don't squash your rice
don't blow your rice
don't wash with your rice

weigh it
stew it
boil it
chew it

I'd love to tackle an apple
apples are the best
throw me a load
then throw me the rest

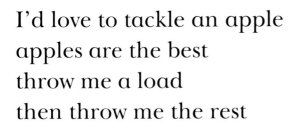

grapple your apple with your fingers
grapple your apple with your thumbs
grapple your apple with some peaches
grapple your apple with some plums

give a bite to a runner
give a bite to a walker
give a bite to a cyclist
give a bite to a talker

apple in a pie
apple on the wall
apple at the dance
apple in the hall

chew two at a picnic
chew two up a tree
chew two at the disco
chew two chew three

don't hide your apple
don't cuddle your apple
don't bowl your apple
don't juggle your apple

polish it
feel it
grip it
peel it

I'm funny about honey
I'm nuts about nuts
I'm awake for cake
I've got the head for bread
I've got the legs for eggs
I want rice in a trice
I dream of ice cream
I'd love to tackle an apple

I'll have it cold
I'll have it hot
I'll have it now
I'll have the lot

I want to shout
I want to roar
I want to yell
I want some more